**THIRTY
DAYS HAS
SEPTEMBER**

Written by Chris Stevens
Illustrated by Sarah Horne
Edited by Liz Scoggins
Designed by Zoe Bradley

THIRTY DAYS HAS SEPTEMBER

Buster Books

This paperback edition of *Thirty Days Has September*
was first published in Great Britain in 2013 by Buster Books,
an imprint of Michael O'Mara Books Limited,
9 Lion Yard, Tremadoc Road, London SW4 7NQ

W www.busterbooks.co.uk   f Buster Children's Books   @BusterBooks

'The Presidents Poem' on page 63 is a recent version of a teacher's mnemonic that has
been used in the United States for many years. Since it has to be updated every four
years, with each presidential election, it is almost certainly the work of several hands. The
author and publishers have made every effort to trace the author(s) of the poem, but
without success, although slightly differing versions of it can be found on many websites.
The version printed here is that found on the website www.homeschoolzone.com,
with two additional lines bringing the poem up to date.

Every reasonable effort has been made to acknowledge all copyright holders. Any errors
or omissions that may have occurred are inadvertent, and anyone with any copyright
queries is invited to write to the publishers, so that a full acknowledgement may be
included in subsequent editions of this work.

A CIP catalogue record for this book is available from the British Library.

ISBN: 978-1-78055-133-3

3 5 7 9 10 8 6 4 2

Printed and bound in November 2013 by CPI Group (UK) Ltd,
108 Beddington Lane, Croydon, CR0 4YY, United Kingdom.

Papers used by Michael O'Mara Books are natural, recyclable products
made from wood grown in sustainable forests. The manufacturing processes
conform to the environmental regulations of the country of origin.

CONTENTS

ALL ABOUT THIS BOOK

Information is easy to remember when you use every trick in the book – well, in this book actually! It's full of really useful memory devices called 'mnemonics'. Some are mental short-cuts, some are catchy rhymes, and there are even some silly jokes, but they are all designed to send quick reminders to your brain.

Acrostics

You'll find lots of sentences where the first letters of each word combine to remind you how to spell another word. These are called 'acrostics'. Here's one that shows you how to spell **M-N-E-M-O-N-I-C**:

Mum **N**eeds **E**ffective **M**ethods **O**r **N**othing **I**s **C**ertain.

Rhymes

There are some unforgettable songs and rhymes to make sure that you can always bring a fact to mind. The title of this book, for example, is part of a rhyme that people use to remember how many days there are in each month of the year (you can read the whole rhyme on page 81).

Acronyms

Acronyms are made up of initials. You probably use acronyms already without even realising it. Do you ever sign off text messages or emails with the letters '**LOL**'? That's an acronym. The letters stand for 'Lots Of Love' or 'Laugh Out Loud'. Did you know that **SCUBA** is an acronym, too? It stands for **S**elf-**C**ontained **U**nderwater **B**reathing **A**pparatus, and **LASER** really means **L**ight **A**mplification by **S**timulation **E**mission of **R**adiation. You'll discover lots more in this book.

Pictures

As you make your way through this book you will come across dozens of clever connections to keep vital information at the tip of your tongue, with pictures to fix the ideas in your mind.

You'll find lots of indispensable tips and hints, such as why you should 'Never Eat Slimy Worms' and what 'Lefty loosey, Righty tighty' reminds you of.

In no time at all you'll be creating your own mnemonics and spotting them yourself.

You'd better clear a space inside your brain – it's about to fill up with fascinating facts!

EXCELLENT ENGLISH

IT'S AS EASY AS
A ... B ... C ...

You will probably find that you already know more mnemonics than you realise. For instance, when you first learnt the alphabet you may have sung the letters to the tune of a well-known song to help you remember the order they come in.

The Alphabet

The letters of the alphabet are often sung to the tune of 'Twinkle, Twinkle, Little Star', like this:

A---B----C---D---E--F--G,
(Twinkle, twinkle, little star,)
H----I---J---K----L-M-N-O-P,
(How I wonder what you are.)
Q-- R S---T---U-------V,
(Up above the world so high,)
W------ -X-------Y------Z.
(Like a diamond in the sky.)
Now I know my ABCs,
(Twinkle, twinkle, little star,)
Next time won't you sing with me?
(How I wonder what you are.)

That's how easy it is to use mnemonics.

Vowels and Consonants

The English alphabet is made up of 26 letters that combine in different ways to make up every word in the entire English language – all 400,000 of them.

Five of the letters are 'vowels', which are soft sounds, and the remaining 21 are harder-sounding letters called 'consonants'.

An easy way to remember that **A**, **E**, **I**, **O** and **U** are the vowels is to use a simple acrostic sentence such as:

Another **E**agle **I**s **O**ver **U**s.

This also reminds you of the order in which the vowels appear in the alphabet.

SORT OUT YOUR SPELLING

There are lots of words that can be tricky to get right. Here are some useful ways to remind you how to spell them. For example, to recall how to spell the word 'accident', you should remember:

'When two **c**ars **c**ollide they make a **dent** – a**cc**ident.'

In this sentence the '**c**'s in the words '**c**ar' and '**c**ollide' serve to remind you that there are two '**c**'s in a**cc**ident, followed by the word '**dent**'.

Accident

When two **c**ars **c**ollide they make a **dent** – a**cc**ident.

Accommodate

Always remember you must a**cc**o**mm**odate two '**c**'s, two '**m**'s and an '**o**' after each.

Address

You should **add** the proper **add**ress for your letter to arrive **s**afe and **s**ound.

Aeroplane

Activate **E**ngines **R**oar **O**ff – **aero**plane.

Argument

The '**e**' in argu**e** always loses in an argument.

Beard

A b**ear**d looks best from **ear** to **ear**.

Beautiful

Big **E**ars **A**ren't **U**gly,
they're **beau**tiful!

Because

Big Elephants Can't Always Understand Small Elephants.

Bicycle

You won't forget how to spell this word, if you remember:

It's best not to use your bi**cy**cle
when it's **icy** on the road.

Breakfast

When you get up and eat breakfast you '**break**' your '**fast**'. (A fast is when you go without food or drink for a time.)

Definite

To remember this tricky one always tell yourself that:

There is definitely no '**a**' in de**finite**.

Difficulty

Mrs **D**, Mrs **I**, Mrs **F F I**, Mrs **C**, Mrs **U**, Mrs **L T Y**.

Embarrass

It's only natural to go **re**ally **r**ed and smile **sh**yly when you are emba**rr**a**ss**ed.

Geography

George **E**dward's **O**ld **G**randmother **R**ode **A** **P**ig **H**ome **Y**esterday – **GEOGRAPHY**.

Grammar

My **Gran**d**ma** uses perfect gram**ma**r.

I Before E

I before **E**, except after **C**,
Or when sounded like **A**,
As in neighbour and weigh.

So it's '**ie**' in 'bel**ie**ve', but '**ei**' in 'rec**ei**ve'. Like many spelling rules there are some pesky exceptions. The 'I before E' rule does not apply to words such as 'ancient' when the '**c**' sounds more like a '**sh**'.

Other common exceptions include 'th**ei**r', and 'w**ei**rd', which, as you can see, don't have the letter '**c**' in them at all, but still use '**ei**'.

Library

Living In Books Really Aids Reading Years.

Lovely

Remind yourself that:

Everyone **love**s
a **love**ly present.

Minute

Many Insects Never Use The Escalator.

Mississippi

Say to yourself, 'M, I, double S, I, double S, I, double P, I'. Or:

Mrs M Mrs I Mrs S S I, Mrs S S I, Mrs P P I.

Necessary

When it's ne**cess**ary to wear a smart shirt remember that it has one **c**ollar and two **s**leeves.

Original

Can you spot the orig**in in** origin**a**l?

Parallel

Parallel lines run alongside each other, an equal distance apart, like train tracks. Imagine the two 'l's in the middle of the word paral**l**el running off into the distance.

People

People **E**at **O**melettes, **P**eople **L**ike **E**ggs.

Possible

I think anything is possible.

Queue

Queen Ursula Eats Up Eggs.

Rhythm

Rhythm Helps Your Two Hips Move.

Separate

Just remember that the two 'a's in this word are separated by the letter 'r'. Or that:

Several Elephants PARAded, Trumpeting Eagerly.

Sincerely

'Since' I 'rely' on honesty,
I must say things sincerely.

Special

The word 'special' can be confusing as it uses the letters 'c', 'i', and 'a' to make the 'sh' sound. Try this mnemonic:

A CIA agent is a special agent.

Succeed

There are only three words in the whole English language that end in 'ceed' – suc**ceed**, pro**ceed**, and ex**ceed**.

If you use two 'c's and two 'e's you will su**ccee**d.

Surprise

Sudden **U**nexpected **R**oars, **P**ings and **R**umbles **I**nduce **S**hock in **E**verybody.

Wednesday

WE Do **N**ot **E**at **S**andwiches on **WEDNES**days.

DON'T HESITATE TO PUNCTUATE

Without punctuation, it would be difficult to know how to read this sentence, wouldn't it? Without commas and full stops telling you when to pause and take a breath you would keep on reading and reading and reading until you ran out of … (gasp) … puff.

So, when you are looking for the end of a sentence, you are usually on a **QUEST** for:

QUestion marks, **E**xclamation marks and full **ST**ops.

So that's clear. Okay? Excellent!

Rules of Punctuation

Here is an updated version of a poem called 'The Rules of Punctuation', which Cecil Hartley wrote in 1818. It explains the old-school rules for reading aloud:

> The stops point out the length of pause
> A reader needs between each clause:
> For every comma, a count of one;
> Then count for two at a semicolon;
> Each colon prefers a count of three;
> A full stop four, we all agree.

Read on to find out how to use all the punctuation marks mentioned in the poem, and more.

Full Stops

A full stop **(.)** ends a sentence. It brings it to a stop.

In the USA and Canada a full stop is known as a 'period', but it always does the same job:

When the sentence is **full**, a **full stop stops** any more words from squeezing in.

If you spot a dot in the middle of a sentence it is most likely there to **stop** you forgetting something. So when a series of words, such as British Broadcasting Corporation, is reduced to its initials like this – B.B.C. – the dots are added after each letter to stop you forgetting the missing letters.

Other dots are used to **stop** you forgetting that letters have been left out of a word. For example, 'Prof.' is short for professor, and 'etc.' is short for etcetera.

Exclamation Marks

A sentence doesn't always have to end in a full stop. To make your writing more exciting, you can finish with a flourish and add an exclamation mark (**!**). It shows that something dramatic has happened. It's an EXCLAMATION!

When the dog bit his finger Max exclaimed, 'Ouch!'

If you think the words you have used sound like an exclamation, it's probably okay to use an exclamation mark.

Top tip: never use more than one exclamation mark. That's bad punctuation!!!

Question Marks

Questions must always end in question marks **(?)**. For example:

'Who threw that stone? What's your name?' asked Sally.

Don't use a question mark when a sentence talks about a question, but doesn't ask it straight out, like this:

Sally wanted to know which boy had broken her window, and what his name was.

Just remember:

Have you asked a question?
Do you need a question mark?

Commas

Commas **(,)** are very useful little things. They can be used to separate items on a list, like this:

We got up, had breakfast, walked to the beach, swam, ate our picnic, built sandcastles, and came home late.

If a sentence is made up of different parts that could easily be used as separate sentences, each part is a 'clause'. For example, this sentence shows two clauses separated by a comma:

It was sunny, so we went to the beach.

It can be split into two separate sentences:

> It was sunny. We went to the beach.

However, instead of splitting the sentence up, a comma has been used with a joining word (called a 'conjunction'), 'so', in the middle. (See page 34 for more on conjunctions.) The comma separates the second clause – the fact that you went to the beach – from the first clause – the fact that it was sunny.

Use this mnemonic to keep the rule in mind:

> What's the difference between a cat and a comma?
> A cat has claws at the ends of its paws
> A comma's a pause at the end of a clause.

Semicolons

A semicolon looks like a full stop on top of a comma (;).
One of the uses of the semicolon is as a way to link up
different clauses instead of using 'and' over and over and
over again. For example:

We got up and had breakfast before going to the beach;
by lunch we'd all had a swim and were ready for a picnic.

Remember this:

A semicolon's **handy** when **and** has been banned.

Colons

A colon looks like one full stop on top of another (:).
It's useful when you want to show that an explanation or a
list is coming. For example, if you want to explain what you
had for your picnic, or why you had a picnic, you might
write:

We packed a picnic: sandwiches, lemonade, boiled eggs,
tomatoes, biscuits, buns and apple pie.

Or:

There were two reasons Mum insisted on packing
a picnic: there is nowhere to buy food at the beach,
and we all get very hungry.

Think of a colon as an: explanation mark.

Hyphens and Dashes

Hyphens **(-)** and dashes **(–)** may look quite similar, but they do different jobs. Hyphens are used to join words together, and dashes are used to break words up. Just remember:

Hyphens hang words together – dashes divide them.

You can use a hyphen to link two words and create new meanings, such as:

'Double-cross' and 'bitter-sweet'.

Use a dash to divide words and to add a stronger pause within a sentence:

He was late – I was angry.

or to interrupt a sentence with some extra information:

He was late – his bus was delayed – and I was angry.

Apostrophes

Possession. Use an apostrophe **(')**, pronounced 'a-poss-tro-fee', to show possession (that something belongs). Add it to the end of a word and follow it with the letter '**s**'.

For example:

> Charlie's dog is chewing Becky's hat.

In this sentence the apostrophe before the 's' is a signal
– it shows you that the word 'Becky' is possessive. She
owns something – a chewed hat.

However, if Charlie's dog decided to chew several hats
belonging to lots of girls, not only would Charlie and his
dog be in even more trouble, but the apostrophe would
have to move to the other side of 's' as well:

> Charlie's dog chewed the girls' hats.

Here's a handy way to remember how to use an apostrophe to show possession:

> Add the apostrophe and then an '**s**'
> To show that something is possessed.
> If the thing has an '**s**' at the end,
> First comes '**s**' then our apostrophe friend.

Omission. When talking, people often say 'you've' instead of 'you have' or 'we'll' instead of 'we will' as it saves time. You should use an apostrophe to show that one or more letters have been deliberately omitted (missed out). For example, Becky might say:

> 'Look at my hat – it's ruined.'

Here are some more examples of words where letters have been missed out:

> 'Do not' becomes 'don't'.
> 'I am' becomes 'I'm'.
> 'Are not' becomes 'aren't'.

To remember the two ways in which you can use an apostrophe, keep this mnemonic in mind:

> A**po**strophes show **p**ossession and **o**mission.

GET TO GRIPS WITH GRAMMAR

Learning English grammar is a bit like shaking hands with an octopus – at first glance it seems impossibly complicated, slippery and hard to grasp. But just as an octopus never gets tied up in knots, you won't either, once you know the basic rules of grammar.

This poem, by an anonymous author, is a good place to start:

Every name is called a **noun**,
As **field** and **fountain**, **street** and **town**.

In place of noun the **pronoun** stands,
As **he** and **she** can clap their hands.

The **adjective** describes a thing,
As **magic** wand and **bridal** ring.

The **verb** means action, something done –
To **read**, to **write**, to **jump**, to **run**.

How things are done, the **adverbs** tell,
As **quickly**, **slowly**, **badly**, **well**.

The **preposition** shows relation,
As **in** the street, or **at** the station.

Conjunctions join, in many ways,
Sentences, words, **or** phrase **and** phrase.

The **interjection** cries out, 'Hark!
I need an exclamation mark!'

Through poetry, we learn how each
Of these makes up the **Parts of Speech**.

Read on to find out more about all the rules of grammar mentioned in the poem and great ways to remember them.

The Parts of Speech

An octopus has eight tentacles, and so does good grammar. Grammar's tentacles are called the 'parts of speech'. They appear on each of the octopus's legs below:

Every word in the English language is attached to one of these eight parts of speech. You don't have to learn every word though. Even Shakespeare only managed to use a small percentage of them (and he invented some of those).

Nouns

A noun is the name of any object: a person, an animal, a thing, an idea or a place. There is a name for everything and that name is a noun.

Question: how many nouns can you find in the following sentence?

Charlie the black dog chases Tibbles the ginger cat up the old tree, sits on the path while he wags his tail happily and barks – 'woof-woof!'

Answer: there are seven nouns – 'Charlie', 'dog', 'Tibbles', 'cat', 'tree', 'path' and 'tail'.

Two are 'proper nouns' – the animals' names, Charlie and Tibbles. The names of things like people, towns and countries are all proper nouns and always start with a capital letter.

The other five nouns are 'common nouns' and don't start with capital letters. Remember:

A **n**oun is a **n**ame.

Adjectives

All these words are adjectives that could probably be used to describe you!

Angelic
Daring
Jolly
Excellent
Clever
Truthful
Inventive
Virtuous
Eccentric

Adjectives usually go immediately in front of the noun they are describing. In the cat-and-dog sentence on the previous page, the dog is black, the cat is ginger and the tree is old. 'Black', 'ginger' and 'old' are all adjectives. So remember:

An **adj**ective is a word used to describe a noun. It tells you more about it – it **ad**ds information to the noun.

Verbs

No sentence is complete without a verb. A verb can be an action word, used to describe what someone or something is doing. For example:

Ben runs, jumps and falls.

A verb can also be a 'being' word, used to describe what someone or something is. For example:

Ben's leg is broken.

These are all verbs:

Vanish, **E**scape, **R**un, **B**olt.

When a verb needs to be more descriptive an 'auxiliary verb' gives a helping hand. These verbs, such as 'to be', 'to do' or 'to have' give extra support to the main verb:

Ben will be running today.
Ben has been jumping.
Ben does not enjoy falling.

So remember:

An auxiliary verb gives extra help to the main verb.

Adverbs

An 'adverb' is used to describe a verb. It **ad**ds information to the verb.

Adverbs are easy to spot because they usually end in the letters 'ly'.

Here are a few adverbs to help you remember:

> **A**thletically
> **D**aintily
> **V**aliantly
> **E**ffortlessly
> **R**ichly
> **B**eautifully

An **ad**verb **ad**ds information to a verb.

Conjunctions

A conjunction, such as 'and', 'or' and 'but', is used to link words, clauses and sentences. It is where they meet – like the **junction** of two roads.

Use this mnemonic to remember the conjunctions:

For, **A**nd, **N**or, **B**ut, **O**r, **Y**et, **S**o (**FAN BOYS!**)

Pronouns

A pronoun, such as 'he', 'she', 'you' or 'it', takes the place of a noun that has already been mentioned. The English language would be cluttered and ugly without them. Imagine talking like this:

> John said that John's mother was taking John in John's mother's car to visit John's mother's friends and see John's mother's friends' goldfish.

Call in the pronouns and try again:

> John said that his mother was taking him in her car to visit her friends and see their goldfish.

> A pronoun is a stand-in, a stunt-man – a **pro**fessional **noun**. It **pro**ps up a **noun** when it is in need of a rest.

The words 'what', 'why', 'when', 'how', 'where', and 'who', which appear in this classic Rudyard Kipling verse, are all adverbs. Two of them – 'what' and 'who' – can also be used as pronouns, as well as for asking questions. Remember:

> I keep six honest serving-men
> (They taught me all I knew);
> Their names are What and Why and When
> And How and Where and Who.

Prepositions

A preposition tells you where to find a noun. 'To', 'in', 'for', 'by', 'into', 'of', 'off', and 'at' are all prepositions. For example:

The cat sat on the grass, in the garden, by the pond.

Remember:

A pre**position** reveals the **position** of a noun.

Interjections

An interjection is a word thrown into a sentence. It doesn't have to link with the other words. For example:

Some interjections are the rudest words in the language. We won't go '**inter**' those or there'll be ob**jections**!

SAME SOUND, DIFFERENT MEANING

Words that sound the same but mean completely different things are known as 'homophones'. For example, 'hear' and 'here' are homophones. It's essential to pick the correct spelling, so that people know exactly what you mean.

Here are some useful ways to remember the different meanings and spellings of some common homophones.

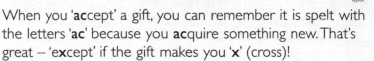

Accept / Except

When you 'accept' a gift, you can remember it is spelt with the letters 'ac' because you acquire something new. That's great – 'except' if the gift makes you 'x' (cross)!

Say this to yourself as a reminder:

'I will accept anything, except excuses!'

Affect / Effect

'Affect' is an action word (a verb). You should use it to say that something makes a difference. For example:

The weather always affects the sailors' ability.

'Effect' is usually an object word (a noun) and is the result of something. For example:

The effect of the weather was terrible.

So remember:

> To affect something alters it,
> But the effect is the end result.

Simpler still, use the 'RAVEN' acronym:

> Remember: Affect, Verb, Effect, Noun.

Allowed / Aloud

When you say something 'aloud', you will know how it is spelt by remembering you say it out **loud**. However, when you are 'allowed' to do something, you have permission to do it.

Aural / Oral

Anything related to your ears is 'aural'. Anything related to your mouth is 'oral'.

Imagine opening your mouth in a huge 'o' as if you are visiting the dentist for your oral health.

Boar / Bore

The word 'b**ore**' has lots of different meanings when it is spelt this way. It can be a noun, used to describe a dull and uninteresting person, or it can be a verb meaning to be dull and uninteresting. It can also describe drilling a hole, or be the width of a gun barrel.

But the word 'b**oar**' can only mean a male pig:

He is **b**ristly, **o**verweight **a**nd **r**eally ugly!

Brake / Break

To remember the difference between these two words, tell yourself:

If you're in a rush, don't forget to 'br**ake**' when you **take** a corner on your bi**ke**.

If you accidentally 'br**eak**' a window it's best to:

Blame **R**eally **E**nergetic **A**ngry **K**angaroos!

Buy / By / Bye

To sort out the differences between these three words, just memorize this sentence.

> I always say **bye bye** when I pass **by**
> on the way to shops to **buy** something.

Capital / Capitol

You can have 'capit**al**' letters and 'capit**al**' cities and **a l**ot of other different meanings.

But the word 'capit**ol**' only has **o**ne. With an '**o**' it's always the g**o**vernment building where laws are made.

Complement / Compliment

A 'compl**i**ment' spelt with the letter '**i**' is a little bit of praise, remember:

> **I** like compliments.

A 'compl**e**ment' with an '**e**' helps to make a thing compl**e**te, for example:

> That shade of gr**ee**n really compl**e**ments
> the colour of your **eye**s.

Chord / Cord

'Cord' is another word for rope. You have vocal cords and a spinal cord, and when you were born the midwife cut your umbilical cord.

However, a group of musical notes played at the same time is called a 'chord' with an 'h'. Remember:

> You can't sing a chord by yourself.
> you need a chorus of friends.

Dear / Deer

To tell these words apart, you should remember that 'dear' is the first word to write in a letter to every auntie.

But a 'deer' is an animal.

Keep this image in mind:

> The deer emerged from the eerie forest.

Desert / Dessert

A 'desert' is full of **s**and, with one '**s**', but a 'de**ss**ert' is a pudding, full of **s**weet **s**tuff, with two '**s**'s.

Dual / Duel

'Dual' is an **a**djective, which means 'two of' or 'double'. Inside the cabin of a jumbo jet there are two sets of controls for two pilots to use:

The word **a**eropl**a**ne has two '**a**'s and dual controls.

A 'duel' is a fight between two people to settle an argument:

A quarr**el** sometimes
ends with a du**el**.

Fair / Fare

'Fair' spelt this way can mean that something is equal and just, or describe something that is quite good, like fair weather. It can also mean light-coloured. If you are blonde, you have **fair hair**.

However, on a bus, passengers pay a '**fare**'. Remember:

To go **f**or **a** **r**ide **e**ach time.

Flour / Flower

The '**flour**' used to bake a cake helps the sponge to rise, but a cake made with '**flowers**' will come out much **lower**!

Grate / Great

A '**grate**' is a part of a fireplace, or it can be a way to shred your food, so:

You'll be glad you **ate** the cheese you gr**ate**d.

You can use the word '**great**' to emphasise how big something is, or to show how much you like it:

Great is **R**eally **E**xcellent **A**ll the **T**ime!

Hear / Here

You '**hear**' with your **ears**, but '**here**' is w**here** you are.

43

Knew / New

A fun way of distinguishing between these two is realising that once you have read this book there'll be **n**othing **n**ew to learn! (Well, almost!) And if anyone asks you a question you'll **k**ick yourself if you forget you **k**new the answer.

Loose / Lose

Remember, if you 'lose' your money, you'll have 'o' (nothing!).

If your trousers are **too** 'loose', they'll fall down.

And if you **loo**sen your belt, you add more 'o's (holes!) to it.

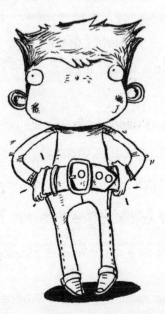

Pair / Pear

A 'pair' spelt like this means that you have two matching items, such as a pair of shoes:

> The perfect **pair** of shoes makes you feel as though you are walking on **air**.

But a p**ear** is a fruit that is delicious to **eat**.

Practice / Practise

Practi**c**e with a '**c**' is a noun, an object word. Practi**s**e with an '**s**' is a verb, an action word. For example:

> **C**olin went to **c**hoir practi**c**e while **S**ue practi**s**ed her **s**axophone.

The letter '**c**' comes before '**s**' in the alphabet, just as '**noun**' comes before '**verb**' in the dictionary.

Principal / Principle

The princi**pal** is the person in charge:

> Make sure the princi**pal** is your **pal**.

A princi**ple** is a law or a guideline to live by, so:

> Stick to your princi**ple**s **ple**ase.

Ring / Wring

People wear **r**ings on their fingers, but **w**ring with a '**w**' means to t**w**ist the **w**ater out of a **w**et cloth.

Stationary / Stationery

A **car** is station**a**ry when it is p**ar**ked.

An **e**nvelope is a piece of station**e**ry.

Their / There / They're

To sort these three words out, remember:

'Th**ei**r' means that something belongs to 'them'. The '**e**' must come first as there is no '**i**' in 'them'. So this common word breaks the 'I before E' spelling rule.

'Th**e**re' is a place. It's here with a '**t**' in front. You go from 'here' to '**t**here'.

'Th**ey**'re', on the other hand, is a shorter way of saying 'they are'. The apostrophe (**'**) in the middle tells you that a letter has been missed out (see page 27 for more on this).

FIGURE OUT THE FIGURES OF SPEECH

Do you always mean what you say? It would be odd if you did. People use language in many clever ways, to convey meaning without 'spelling it out'.

Metaphor

In the sentence above 'spelling it out' is a figure of speech. Did you notice? In this case, to 'spell out' is an expression used to mean a slow, careful, clear description. It does not literally mean s-p-e-l-l-i-n-g i-t o-u-t. It is a 'metaphor' (pronounced met-uh-for).

What's a metaphor? For getting your ideas across. In Ancient Greek it meant 'to transfer' – you can use metaphors to transfer meaning from one thing to another.

For instance, when people say 'it's raining cats and dogs', they don't literally mean that cats and dogs are falling from the sky, they just mean that it's raining heavily. The metaphor makes the rain sound much more interesting.

Use this as a reminder:

I **met a** friend **phor** tea. She is such a star.

(Remember that your friend isn't literally a star in the sky, or even a film star, but she does have some wonderful qualities.)

47

Similes

A 'simile' (pronounced sim-ill-ee) makes a link between two ideas and emphasizes it by saying one is 'like' the other:

'My love is **like** a red, red rose,' is a simile.
'Your nose is **as** red **as** a beetroot,' is a simile, too.

Remember:

Similes usually use '**as**' or '**like**' – another word for **simil**ar.

Alliteration

'Alliteration' means that several words in a sentence start with the same letter or sound – see? Remember:

Alliteration is littered with letters.

Next time you are on a long car journey, why not take turns to invent a sentence of alliteration for each letter of the alphabet? Some are easy – 'Peter Piper picked a peck of pickled peppers' – some might seem almost impossible – 'Quick quilters quietly quarrelled over a quince'.

Assonance

With 'assonance', either the vowels can rhyme, but not the consonants (as in tide and find), or the consonants can match, but not the vowels (as in **mast** and **mist**).

Remember this example:

> As the tide rises the sailors find that
> the ship's **mast** is **most**ly hidden by **mist**.

Onomatopoeia

'Onomatopoeia' (pronounced on-o-mat-uh-pee-a) is the use of words that sound like the thing they describe, such as 'crunch', 'plink', and 'boing'. Imagine trying to write the noise that a duck makes – you might well write 'quack'.

It's a hard word even to remember how to say, let alone spell, so imagine yourself whacking a jangling gong, '**on a mat**, on **a pier**':

PUTTING IT INTO PRACTICE

Here are some top tips to help you put your new-found knowledge to good use.

Storytelling

Once you have mastered grammar, punctuation and figures of speech, you'll soon be ready to make a start on your first book! If you need some help, just imagine these six people appearing in a story together:

> **P**rince Charming
> **C**inderella
> **S**now White
> **M**iss Muffet
> **F**riar Tuck
> **T**om Thumb

They are a mixed bunch of characters, but their first initials stand for the six essential elements of great storytelling:

Plot, **C**haracters, **S**etting, **M**ood, **F**ocus and **T**heme.

Plot. This is your storyline. You should have a beginning, a middle and an end. It keeps the audience asking, 'What happens next?'

Characters. Describe the appearance, characteristics, emotions and experiences of the people involved in your story to make them lifelike.

Setting. Whether you're inventing a fantasy world,

describing a place you know really well, or imagining a time in history you'd love to visit, make sure that your setting seems real.

Mood. If you're telling a tragic tale, don't spoil things by peppering it with puns and jokes. A comic story needs a happy ending, or your audience will feel betrayed.

Focus. It will be confusing if you hop around from one character to another. Choose just one or two to focus on and tell the story from their point of view.

Theme. What's it all about? If your story is more than just random events that happen to unimportant people, the tale will have a theme. It will mean something, with a message your audience will remember. For example, your story could be about friendship, or football, or even fame.

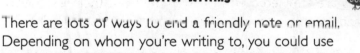

Letter Writing

There are lots of ways to end a friendly note or email. Depending on whom you're writing to, you could use anything from 'Kind regards' to 'Love and kisses'.

But if you are ending a formal letter, there are rules. 'Yours sincerely' means you are writing to a person you've met or spoken with before. 'Yours faithfully' means you are writing to someone you don't know at all.

Remember it with this rhyme:

> **Since** we spoke I'm yours **since**rely …
> Faithfully – we've never met (clearly).

HOT ON HISTORY

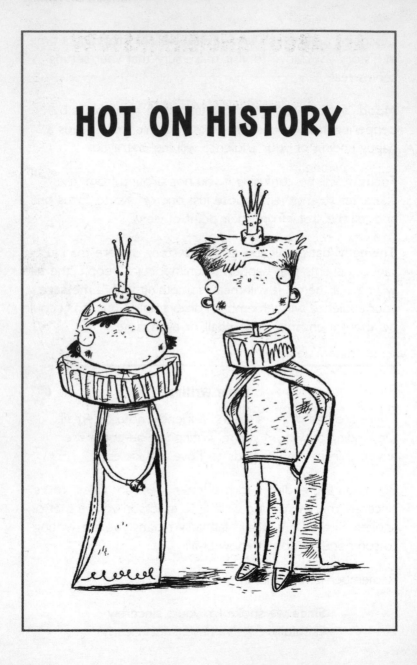

ALL ABOUT ANCIENT HISTORY

The Seven Wonders of the World

Tourism is nothing new. The Ancient Greeks made a list of the best sights to visit around the Mediterranean.

We know these sights as the 'Seven Wonders of the Ancient World'. Sadly, only the Great Pyramid of Giza still survives for you to visit today.

Making up a story is an excellent way to memorize a list of information. For example, picture yourself on a whirlwind week of sightseeing through history – imagine the noises, smells and sights you would see – to make the list of 'wonders' easier to remember.

Tell yourself this story a few times or, if you prefer, make up one of your own:

On Monday I meandered through the Mausoleum of Maussollos.

On Tuesday I took in the Temple of Artemis before tea.

Wednesday's wonder was the
Lighthouse of Alexandria.

On Thursday I hung out in the
Hanging Gardens of Babylon.

Friday finished with the famous
Colossus of Rhodes.

On Saturday I saw the
Statue of Zeus at Olympia.

On Sunday I sailed up the river Nile
to see the Great Pyramid of Giza.

The Greek Alphabet

Try this challenging tongue twister to learn the letters
of the Greek alphabet:

This is Greek and how they spelt her,
Alpha, Beta, Gamma, Delta,
Epsilon, Zeta,
Eta, Theta,
Then Iota, Kappa too,
Followed up by Lambda, Mu.

Nu, Xi,
Omicron, Pi,
After that, Rho, Sigma, Tau,
Upsilon, Phi, and still three more,
Chi, Psi, and Omega makes twenty-four.

Philosophers

Ancient Greek philosophers were great thinkers whose ideas helped to guide people through everyday life.

The initials of the most important Ancient Greek philosophers spell out the word '**SPA**'. They were:

> **S**ocrates (469 – 399 BC)
> **P**lato (c.429 – c.347 BC)
> **A**ristotle (384 – 322 BC).

Another way to remember all three Ancient Greek philosophers is to think that they were important because they were:

> **So PopulAr.**

Roman Emperors

Most people have heard of Julius Caesar, the first Emperor of Rome, but after he was killed there were five more 'Caesars':

Augustus	(31 BC – AD 14)
Tiberius	(AD 14 – AD 37)
Caligula	(AD 37 – AD 41)
Claudius	(AD 41 – AD 54)
Nero	(AD 54 – AD 68).

Impress your classmates by committing them to memory with this sentence:

BE THE BEST
AT BRITISH HISTORY

Kings and Queens

A great way to make history easier is to learn or invent a rhyme. This one about the kings and queens of England has been around for a long time:

> Willie, Willie, Harry, Stee,
> Harry, Dick, John, Harry Three,
> One, Two, Three Neds, Richard Two,
> Harrys Four, Five, Six ... then who?
>
> Edwards Four, Five, Dick the Bad,
> Harry twice, Ed Six the lad,
> Mary, Bessie, James you ken,
> Charlie, Charlie, James again,
>
> Will and Mary, Anne of gloria,
> George times Four, Will Four, Victoria,
> Edward Seven next, and then
> Came George the Fifth in 1910.
>
> Ned the Eighth soon abdicated
> So George Six was coronated,
> Then number two Elizabeth,
> Next Charles the Third ... I'm out of breath!

Did you notice that little bit of Scots, 'James you ken'? It means 'James, you know' and it reminds us that James I was also James VI of Scotland.

If you'd like to know exactly who these people were, and when they reigned, here is the complete list. You'll probably agree this list would be harder to learn than the poem!

William I 'The Conquerer'		Edward VI	(1547 – 1553)
	(1066 – 1087)	Mary I	(1553 – 1558)
William II 'Rufus'	(1087 – 1100)	Elizabeth I	(1558 – 1603)
Henry I	(1100 – 1135)	James I (and VI of Scotland)	
Stephen	(1135 – 1154)		(1603 – 1625)
Henry II	(1154 – 1189)	Charles I	(1625 – 1649)
Richard I 'The Lionheart'		Charles II	(1660 – 1685)
	(1189 – 1199)	James II (and VII of Scotland)	
John	(1199 – 1216)		(1685 – 1688)
Henry III	(1216 – 1272)	William III and Mary II	
Edward I	(1272 – 1307)		(1689 – 1694)
Edward II	(1307 – 1327)	William III	(1694 – 1702)
Edward III	(1327 – 1377)	Anne	(1702 – 1714)
Richard II	(1377 – 1399)	George I	(1714 – 1727)
Henry IV	(1399 – 1413)	George II	(1727 – 1760)
Henry V	(1413 – 1422)	George III	(1760 – 1820)
Henry VI	(1422 – 1461	George IV	(1820 – 1830)
	and 1470 – 1471)	William IV	(1830 – 1837)
Edward IV	(1461 – 1470	Victoria	(1837 – 1901)
	and 1471 – 1483)	Edward VII	(1901 – 1910)
Edward V	(1483)	George V	(1910 – 1936)
Richard III	(1483 – 1485)	Edward VIII	(1936)
Henry VII	(1485 – 1509)	George VI	(1936 – 1952)
Henry VIII	(1509 – 1547)	Elizabeth II	(1952 – present).

Henry VIII

Can you guess which famous women this rhyme refers to?

Kate 'n' Anne 'n' Jane, 'n' Anne 'n' Kate again 'n' again!

They are the six wives of Henry VIII, who was King of England from 1509 to 1547. Their proper names were Catherine of Aragon, Anne Boleyn, and Jane Seymour, followed by Anne of Cleves, Catherine Howard and lastly, Katherine Parr.

And here's how each of Henry's wives met her end:

Divorced, beheaded, died;
Divorced, beheaded, survived.

Royal Houses

Over the last thousand years the main royal families to have ruled over England are:

Norman	(1066 – 1135)
Plantagenet	(1154 – 1399)
Lancaster	(1399 – 1461 and 1470 – 1471)
York	(1461 – 1470 and 1471 – 1485)
Tudor	(1485 – 1603)
Stuart	(1603 – 1649 and 1660 – 1714)
Hanover	(1714 – 1901)
Windsor	(1901 – present day).

Use the first letter of each word in the following sentence as a reminder of the names:

No **P**oint **L**etting **Y**our **T**rousers **S**lip **H**alf **W**ay.

The Wars of the Roses

The Wars of the Roses were a series of twelve battles fought to decide who should be in control of the throne of England. They took place between 1455 and 1487. But it doesn't have to be a battle to learn about them, just use the initials of each word in this sentence to remind you:

A Boy **N**ow **W**ill **M**ention **A**ll **T**he **H**ot **H**orrid **B**attles **T**ill **B**osworth.

The initials not only serve to remind you of the names of

the battles between the sides of York (whose symbol was a white rose) and Lancaster (whose symbol was a red rose), but also to help you recall the order of the battles. They were:

St **A**lbans
Blore Heath
Northampton
Wakefield
Mortimer's Cross
St **A**lbans
Towton
Hedgeley Moor
Hexham
Barnet
Tewkesbury
Bosworth.

If you're a football fan, it's easy to remember which army had which rose. Manchester United, on the Lancashire side, play in red – Leeds United, in Yorkshire, play in white.

The Gunpowder Plot

Here is an extract from a poem that gives one of the most famous mnemonics of them all:

> Remember, remember, the fifth of November,
> Gunpowder, treason and plot.

This reminds us that the 5th of November is Bonfire Night, a celebration that the plot by Guy Fawkes and others to blow up the Houses of Parliament, was foiled in 1605.

MASTER AMERICAN HISTORY

The Discovery of America

Most people now agree that European settlers reached the shores of North America much earlier than Columbus in the 15th century. In fact, Icelandic tales show that one of the earliest settlers, Leif Eriksson the Lucky, reached what may have been Newfoundland more than 400 years sooner.

This poetic extract reminds us of the date that Christopher Columbus eventually arrived in the West Indies – 1492:

> In fourteen hundred and ninety-two,
> Columbus sailed the ocean blue.

The Pilgrim Fathers

The first American colonists, known as the Pilgrim Fathers, sailed to North America on a ship called the Mayflower, in 1620. So remember this:

> It's twenty past four,
> Let's go ashore!

On a 24-hour clock, you'll know that 16:20 means twenty-past-four in the afternoon, and that is guaranteed to jog your memory of this important date.

American Presidents

To date there have been more than forty presidents of the
United States, which is a lot to keep in mind. This rhyme, by
an unknown poet, lists each of the presidents in sequence.
A couple of extra lines have been added to bring things
right up to the present day:

George Washington leads them, the great and the true,
John Adams succeeds him and Jefferson too;
Madison follows, and fifth comes Monroe,
With John Quincy Adams and Jackson below.

The term of Van Buren to Harrison's leads;
Tyler, Polk, Taylor, then Fillmore succeeds.
Pierce and Buchanan, and Lincoln in turn,
Is followed by Johnson and Grant, we discern.

Hayes, Garfield, and Arthur, and Cleveland we score,
Then Harrison is followed by Cleveland once more.
Then comes McKinley and the full dinner pail,
And one called 'Teddy' who to Cuba did sail.

William Taft his government began
And Woodrow Wilson, a marvellous man;
Harding and Coolidge are next in the rhyme,
Then Hoover and the people had a very hard time.

FDR was great in both peace and war,
Truman was striving for what we were fighting for.
The former General Eisenhower
Brought the Republicans back to power.

John Kennedy's victory in the race
Was for the New Frontier in the Age of Space.
Lyndon Johnson led the people, the free and the brave,
With a goal to achieve and a country to save.

Nixon swore to uphold our creed
Of liberty, life and every man's need.
But by Nixon these rules were ignored,
So to take his place was President Ford.

Then came Carter with a cheery smile,
To run our country 'Southern Style'.
Then Carter's smile left his face,
And Reagan came to take his place.

'Dutch' stayed two terms, Bush filled his station,
Bringing with him a 'kinder, gentler nation'.
Clinton took over and served for eight years,
George W followed, with Texan cheers.

Mount Rushmore National Memorial

A massive sculpture of four great American presidents is carved into the rock face of Mount Rushmore in South Dakota, USA. It was sculpted between 1927 and 1941. The heads of George Washington, Thomas Jefferson, Abraham Lincoln and Theodore Roosevelt are each 18 metres high. Remember them with this mnemonic:

> **W**e **J**ust **L**ike **R**ushmore.
> **W**ashington, **J**efferson, **L**incoln, **R**oosevelt.

Great Dates in History

Lots of significant dates have a useful habit of ending in the number six. This makes them much easier to remember:

1066 – The Battle of Hastings
1666 – The Great Fire of London
1776 – The American Declaration of Independence
1966 – The only time the England football team has ever won the World Cup!

GEOGRAPHY GENIUS

Points of the Compass

Any good scout will tell you that it's essential to know which direction is which. You need a compass to tell you north, but then you'll be able to work out which way is east, south and west.

Imagine a compass as the face of a clock – with north, east, south and west running, like the time, in a clockwise direction. North is at 12 o'clock, east is at 3 o'clock, south is at 6 o'clock and west is at 9 o'clock. All these mnemonics will help you remember the right order – so take your pick:

> Never Eat Shredded Wheat
> Never Eat Slimy Worms
> Never Eat Soggy Waffles
> Naughty Elephants Squirt Water
> Never Enter Santa's Workshop.

Map Reading

You can pinpoint any spot in Britain using a six-figure grid reference number. On 'Ordnance Survey' maps, the whole country is divided into boxes, each 100 kilometres square. These boxes are then divided into one hundred smaller squares, with numbers for 'Eastings', running west to east, and 'Northings', running south to north.

With a six-figure grid reference number such as '654321' the first group of numbers (654) refers to the boxes that run across the map – the second (321) refers to boxes that run up the map. So the '6' tells you how far across the map to look and the '3' tells you how far up to look – the '54' and '21' give you more exact locations in each direction. Remember:

Onwards and upwards.

Continents

The world is divided into seven large areas of land, called 'continents' – these are North America, South America, Australia, Antarctica, Africa, Asia, and Europe. Travelling around the world to the tune of 'Frère Jacques' is a great way to remember them:

> North America, South America,
> *(Frère Jacques, Frère Jacques,)*
> Australia, Australia,
> *(Dormez vous? Dormez vous?)*
> Don't forget Antarctica,
> *(Sonnez les matines,)*
> Africa and Asia,
> *(Sonnez les matines,)*
> And Europe, and Europe.
> *(Din, dan, don, din, dan, don.)*

If you'd rather memorize the continents without bursting into song, try these memory boosters for Europe, Asia, Africa, Australia, Antarctica, North America and South America:

> **E**at **A**n **A**pple
> **A**s **A** **N**ice **S**nack.

Or for Asia, Africa, Antarctica, Europe, Australia, North America and South America:

> **A**ll **A**verage **A**nteaters **E**njoy
> **A**nts ... **N**ot **A**unts, I **S**aid **A**nts.

Oceans

The five great world oceans are the Pacific, Atlantic, Indian, Antarctic and the Arctic.

The largest ocean is the Pacific, covering roughly a third of the planet's surface between the Americas and Asia. The world's smallest ocean, the Arctic, covers just two per cent of the Earth's surface in comparison.

To remember the oceans from smallest to largest:

Arctic ants **ind**ulge in **atla**ses, **pa**rticularly.

Or just as a quick reminder in no particular order:

I Am **A**n **A**mazing **P**erson!

The Great Lakes

Between them, the five Great Lakes of North America hold twenty per cent of the fresh water on the surface of the planet. On the border of the United States and Canada from west to east, they are: **S**uperior, **H**uron, **M**ichigan, **E**rie and **O**ntario. Or:

Sam's **H**orse **M**ust **E**at **O**ats.

And if you just need a reminder of the names, not the geography, their initials spell out '**HOMES**'.

Mountains

The top-three tallest mountains in the world are in the Himalayan mountain range between China, India and Nepal. They are:

Everest   8,850 metres high
K2   8,610 metres high
Kangchenjunga   8,586 metres high.

You'll impress your teachers if you can list them in order, but if you can't recall them very easily, use this funny mnemonic as a prompt:

Rivers of the World

The planet's top three longest rivers are:

The **N**ile	6650 kilometres long
The **A**mazon	6400 kilometres long
The **Y**angtze	6300 kilometres long.

It's difficult to get anyone to agree on their exact length, so the measurements given here are not precise. But at least you'll be able to think of their names quickly – just say '**NAY**'.

Deserts

The world's largest hot desert areas are:

The **S**ahara	8,600,000 square kilometres
The **A**rabian	2,300,000 square kilometres
The **G**obi	1,300,000 square kilometres.

Their initials spell out the word '**SAG**'.

Longitude and Latitude

The criss-crossing lines on a map of the world are called lines of 'longitude' and 'latitude'. The long lines that run from North Pole to South Pole are all the same length and are called lines of longitude. Remember:

Lines of **long**itude are all as **long** as one another.

The parallel lines that run around the Earth, like hoops, are lines of latitude. They are all different lengths, and the equator, at 0 degrees, is the one around the middle where the Earth is fattest. Remember:

Lat = fat.

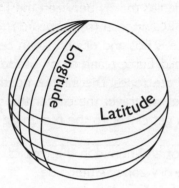

The Tropics of Cancer and Capricorn

The 21st of June is the first day of summer in the northern hemisphere and the first day of winter in the southern hemisphere. At noon on that day the sun is directly overhead at 23.5 degrees north of the equator. This line of latitude is called the 'Tropic of Cancer'.

In the southern hemisphere, December 21st is the first day of summer and in the northern hemisphere it is the first day of winter. At 23.5 degrees south of the equator the sun is directly overhead at midday. This line of latitude is called the 'Tropic of Capricorn'. Remember that:

Cancer is north of the equator –
Capricorn is on the other side.

Climate

The world can be divided into five main climate zones. These are: tropical, dry, temperate, cold and polar.

The tropical zone lies mainly between the Tropic of Cancer and the Tropic of Capricorn (see page 73). To the north and south the climate is hot and dry, but then becomes more temperate, or mild. Europe and much of the United States lie in the temperate zones. The further north or south of the tropical zone you travel, the colder the climate becomes as you get closer to the North or South Pole:

> It's hot and humid in the tropics,
> With dry zones either side.
> Soon you'll find it's temperate,
> Then cold will conquer mild.
> When you reach the polar waste,
> You'd better get inside with haste!

To help you remember, imagine a person, wrapped up in layers of jumpers, but with bare feet and a bare head. They will be hot in the middle, but cold at the top and bottom, just like the world's climate!

American States

This anonymous poem to help you memorize each of the fifty states in America doesn't just rhyme, it's also in alphabetical order:

Alabama and Alaska, Arizona, Arkansas,
California, Colorado, and Connecticut and more.
Delaware, Florida, Georgia, Hawaii, and Idaho.
Illinois, Indiana, Iowa, still 35 to go.

Kansas and Kentucky, Louisiana, Maine.
Maryland, Massachusetts, and good ole Michigan.
Minnesota, Mississippi, Missouri, and Montana,
Nebraska's 27, number 28's Nevada.

Next, New Hampshire and New Jersey,
And way down, New Mexico.
Then New York, North Carolina,
North Dakota, O-Hi-O.

Oklahoma, Oregon, Pennsylvania, now let's see.
Rhode Island, South Carolina, South Dakota, Tennessee.
There's Texas, then there's Utah.
Vermont, I'm almost through.

Virginia, then there's Washington and West Virginia, too.
Could Wisconsin be the last one in the 49?
No, Wyoming is the last state in the 50 states that rhyme.

Phew!

Central American Countries

What lies between North America and South America? Central America, of course. Directly below the United States is **M**exico, followed by the Central American countries of **G**uatemala and **B**elize, **E**l Salvador and **H**onduras, then **N**icaragua, **C**osta **R**ica and **P**anama, leading down to meet South America. Remember:

My **G**reat **B**ig **E**lephant **H**as **N**o **CR**itical **P**roblems.

Imagine the shape of an elephant's trunk to remind you of the mnemonic as well as the shape the countries make as they join the two continents together.

Stalactites and Stalagmites

In caves formed in areas of limestone rock, drips of water seeping through from the ground above gradually develop into long spikes of stone that hang from the ceiling. Where the water drips onto the ground, more spikes build up. These two types of spike have different names – 'stalactites' and 'stalagmites' – but which is which? Just think:

Stala**c**tites **c**ome down from the **c**eiling,
Stala**g**mites **g**row up from the **g**round.

Stalac**tites** stick **'tight'** to the ceiling.
Stalag**mites might** one day reach up to touch them.

And if you imagine what would happen if tiny insects crawled up your aunty's legs:

The '**mites** go up and the '**tites** come down!

Geology

Planet Earth has existed for several billion years, so to describe different lengths of time, geologists use 'aeons', 'eras', 'periods', 'epochs' and 'ages'.

Dinosaurs lived throughout the Triassic, Jurassic and Cretaceous periods, but human beings have only been around since the end of the Tertiary period.

The eleven main geological periods, from the Cambrian – when plant and animal life began to develop more rapidly – to the present day are:

Cambrian:	570 – 510 million years ago
Ordovician:	510 – 440 million years ago
Silurian:	440 – 410 million years ago
Devonian:	410 – 360 million years ago
Carboniferous:	360 – 290 million years ago
Permian:	290 – 245 million years ago
Triassic:	245 – 210 million years ago
Jurassic:	210 – 145 million years ago
Cretaceous:	145 – 65 million years ago
Tertiary:	65 – 1.7 million years ago
Quaternary:	1.7 million years ago – present.

To remember the order from past to present, try this sentence:

Can Ordinary Students Date Carbon Perfectly, Then Join Courses? Tough Question!

Prehistoric Man

The period of time before the written word was developed is known as 'prehistory', as people had no way of recording events as they happened. Early prehistoric man began to use tools made out of stone. This is the period known as the 'Stone Age'.

The three prehistoric eras of Stone Age mankind are:

Palaeolithic, Mesolithic and Neolithic.

Picture a Stone-Age family – **P**a, **M**a and the **N**ew baby.

In many parts of the world the Stone Age was followed by a Bronze Age and an Iron Age, as humans developed more sophisticated methods of tool-making.

TIME,
WEATHER
AND SCIENCE

CALENDAR COUNTDOWN

Keeping track of days and dates can be tricky if you can never remember which months have 30 days and which have 31. Then there's even a month that sometimes has 28 and sometimes has 29 days.

It's so confusing, how will you ever be able to tell how many days you have to wait until your next birthday?

Days of the Month

Use the timeless rhyme that inspired the title of this book to remind you how many days there are in each month of the year.

> Thirty days have September,
> April, June and November.
> All the rest have thirty-one
> Excepting February alone,
> And that has twenty-eight days clear,
> With twenty-nine in each leap year.

For those of you who are more mathematically minded, here is a number-based rhyme that will help you to remember the same thing:

> Fourth, eleventh, ninth and sixth,
> Thirty days to each affix;
> Every other thirty-one,
> Except the second month alone.

If you find it difficult to memorize rhymes, just use your hands for a quick visual reminder.

Hold out both hands in front of you, as shown below. Each of your knuckles represents a month which is 31 days long. The dips between each knuckle represent the months that have only 30 days, except for February, which has 28, or 29 in a leap year, of course.

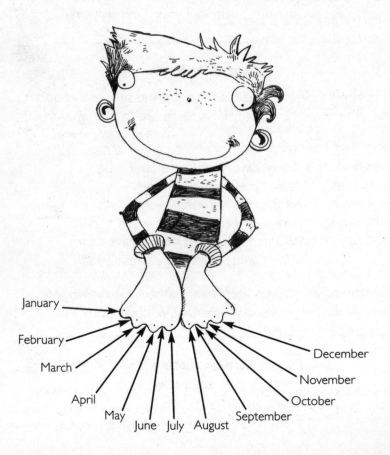

January

February

March

April

May

June

July

August

September

October

November

December

Leap Years

Everyone knows that a normal year is 365 days long, but did you know that it actually takes 365.24 days for the Earth to travel around the Sun?

Happy 4th Birthday

A 'leap' year of 366 days is used every four years to balance out this extra quarter day. So in a leap year February has an extra day, giving it 29 days instead of 28.

Just imagine if you were born on the 29th February. When would you celebrate your birthday? It would be seriously tough to only have a birthday once every four years. When you were 12 in normal years you would have only had four birthday parties!

You can use your four times table to remember when each leap year falls – so far this century they have been 2004 and 2008, then 2012, 2016, 2020 and 2024.

Hurricane Season

If you live in the southern United States or the Caribbean, you won't need to be told that hurricane season lasts throughout the summer. But if you're planning a holiday there be warned: it can get very windy between June and October!

83

The worst months are highlighted by these five separate rhymes:

> June – too soon (for the worst storms).
> July – stand by (the real hurricanes are coming).
> August – you must (be prepared for a battering).
> September – remember (it isn't finished yet).
> October – all over (until next year).

Changing the Clocks

In many countries, the clocks are altered twice a year. This helps people make the most of long summer days, by getting them out of bed earlier.

In Britain, summer time officially begins at 1am on the last Sunday in March, and ends at 1am on the last Sunday in October. So once a year people put clocks forward an hour and once a year they put them back again.

An easy reminder is that the clocks move ahead before they turn back: one step forward, one step back. In the United States autumn is called 'fall', which is why they say:

> Spring Forward, Fall Back.

Or try this memorable rhyme:

> Forward in March, back after September
> And that is all you need to remember!

International Travel

The world is divided into several time zones so that, as the Sun rises in the east, it becomes morning in easterly countries first. By the time it's afternoon in Moscow, it isn't even dawn in New York. So, if you're travelling around the world you'll need to adjust your watch.

If you fly east to west from Europe to America you'll actually gain a few hours because you are moving back through the day. Travelling back in the opposite direction, the hours will disappear as you move forward through the day. Remember that:

> East to west gains.
> West to east loses.

Colours of the Rainbow

An easy way to recall the colours of a rainbow and the order in which they appear is to remember this sentence:

Richard **O**f **Y**ork **G**ave **B**attle **I**n **V**ain.

This acrostic refers to Richard of York who was defeated at the Battle of Bosworth, in England (see page 61). The first letters of each word stand for the following colours: **R**ed, **O**range, **Y**ellow, **G**reen, **B**lue, **I**ndigo and **V**iolet.

Temperature

When you're watching the weather forecast, the following rhyme reminds you what the numbers in Celsius mean.

30°C is hot, 20°C is nice
10°C is cold, 0°C is ice.

MAD ABOUT ASTRONOMY

Astronomers are scientists who study the stars and planets in the night sky. All you need to get started is a cloudless night and you never know where it might take you.

Here are some useful mnemonics to get you started.

The Solar System

The planets in the solar system, in order of their distance from the Sun are:

> Mercury, Venus, Earth, Mars, Jupiter, Saturn, Uranus, Neptune and Pluto.

There are countless memorable mnemonics to remind you of them, including:

> My Very Energetic Monkey Jumped Straight Up Napoleon's Pants!

Unfortunately, to be exact about it, Pluto is no longer classed as a planet. In August 2006, the International Astronomical Union demoted it from 'planet' to 'dwarf planet', so try this acrostic instead:

> My Very Educated Mother Just Served Us Noodles.

The Planets in Size Order

The planets in order of size, from largest to smallest, are:

Jupiter, Saturn, Uranus, Neptune,
Earth, Venus, Mars, Mercury, Pluto.

Remember them with this silly sentence:

Jack Stood Under
Ninety-Eight Vicious
Martian-Munching
Penguins.

Brightest Stars

What's the brightest star in the sky? The Sun, of course. But at night, it's Sirius, The Dog Star, which can be found in the 'constellation' (group of stars) known as Canis Major. It gets its name from 'canis', the Latin word for dog.

Here are the nine brightest stars visible from Earth and the constellations they belong to:

Sirius, in Canis Major
Canopus, in Carina
Rigil Kent, in Centaurus
Arcturus, in Bootes
Vega, in Lyra
Capella, in Auriga
Rigel, in Orion
Procyon, in Canis Major
Achernar, in Eridanus.

This gives you another useful sentence to remember:

Sir can rig a VCR, Pa.

The Moon Landing

The first man to walk on the moon was Neil Armstrong.
He stepped out of the Apollo 11 spacecraft on July 20th,
1969, with the words:

*'That's one small step for a man ...
One giant leap for mankind.'*

His fellow astronaut, Buzz Aldrin,
followed him, but the third man of the
crew, Michael Collins, had to stay behind
to operate the controls. Imagine going
all the way to the moon, but not being
able to get out for a walk around!

Spell 'Apo11o' with '1's instead of 'l's and
you'll never forget the number – and
remembering **A**rmstrong, **B**uzz and
Collins is as easy as '**A, B, C**'.

SUPER SCIENCE

Try these mnemonics as a brief introduction to the worlds of chemistry and biology.

Chemical Formulae

Everything in the universe consists of atoms, and all atoms consist of three components:

Protons
Electrons
Neutrons.

Remember to write that down with your '**PEN**'.

Atoms combine to make more complex substances. These combinations of atoms are called 'molecules'.

For example, two hydrogen atoms (**H**) and an oxygen atom (**O**) together make a molecule known as 'H_2O', which is simply water. Whereas two hydrogen, one sulphur (**S**) and four oxygen atoms combine to make 'H_2SO_4', which is sulphuric acid.

Water and sulphuric acid are very different. Sulphuric acid will burn through just about anything, which is why all budding scientists know this silly rhyme:

> Johnny was a scientist,
> Johnny is no more,
> For what he thought was H_2O, was H_2SO_4.

Biological Classification

The animal and plant world is divided into seven basic categories, each one within the last, like a series of boxes:

> **K**ingdom
> **P**hylum
> **C**lass
> **O**rder
> **F**amily
> **G**enus
> **S**pecies.

Try this reminder to help you think of the order:

> **K**ind **P**eople **C**an
> **O**ccasionally **F**eel
> **G**rumpy **S**uddenly.

So what would 'animalia, chordata, mammalia, carnivora, canidae, canis, canis lupus' be?

A pet dog, of course!

MAGNIFICENT MATHS

NEVER FORGET NUMBERS

Pick a number

When you first learned to count, you probably used a rhyme like this:

One, two, three, four, five.
Once I caught a fish alive.
Six, seven, eight, nine, ten.
Then I let it go again.
Why did you let it go?
Because it bit my finger so.
Which finger did it bite?
This little finger on my right.

From there you will have discovered adding, subtracting, multiplication, division, and more. Now a mathematical mnemonic can help you just as much as counting rhymes did when you were younger.

Here are some simple ways to help you with Roman numerals, times tables and types of triangle.

Roman Numerals

In Ancient Rome numbers were written out as letters. Only the numbers one, five, ten, fifty, one hundred, five hundred and one thousand were used. Any other number would be written by combining these. Here's how it works:

One	I
Five	V
Ten	X
Fifty	L
One hundred	C
Five hundred	D
One thousand	M

Small numbers placed in front of a larger number subtract from it. If they appear after a larger number, they add to it.

So the letters 'VC' mean five (V) less than one hundred (C): 95. 'CV' means five more than one hundred: 105. Here's a mnemonic to keep your Roman numerals in order:

I Value X-rays – Lucy Can't Drink Milk.

TAKE ON YOUR TABLES

Remembering some times tables can be troublesome. The two, the five and the ten times table are easier to learn, but what about the stinky sevens and the nasty nines?

When tackling tables remember that, just as large numbers are made up of smaller numbers, large calculations can be worked out using smaller calculations. Here are some tricks to help you manage those terrible tables in no time at all.

Threes

A quick way of doing your three times table is to treble the number you need to multiply. To do this, multiply it by two, then add the original number to the total:

$$8 \times 3 \text{ is the same as } 8 \times 2 + 8$$
$$8 \times 2 = 16$$
$$16 + 8 = 24$$

The numbers in your total will always add up to 3, 6 or 9.

Fours

For your four times table just remember all those four-legged animals going into Noah's ark – two by two. All you have to do is multiply the number by 2, and then by 2 again. Your total will always be an even number.

$$4 \times 7 \text{ is the same as } 7 \times 2 \times 2$$
$$7 \times 2 = 14$$
$$14 \times 2 = 28$$

Sixes

An easy way to do your six times table is to multiply the number by five, and then add the number to the total:

8 × 6 is the same as 8 × 5 + 8, so
8 × 5 = 40
40 + 8 = 48

Sevens

You can use your two times table and your five times table to work out your sevens, because 2 + 5 = 7. So just remember:

Stinky sevens are simple,
When you know your twos and fives.

For example, to work out 2 × 7 break it down like this:

2 × **2** = 4 and 2 × **5** = 10
so, 4 + 10 = 14

Next time your teacher asks you what the answer to 5 × 7 is, give this method a try:

5 × **2** = 10 and 5 × **5** = 25
so, 10 + 25 = 35

This means that 5 × 7 = 35.

Eights

If you get seriously stuck on your eight times table, here's a way of making it easier:

> If your eights irritate, do the 'double'.

This means eights are easy if you just double the number you want to multiply by eight – once, twice, three times.

For example, to work out 5 × 8, get doubling:

> Double the 5 to get 10.
> Then double the 10 to get 20.
> Then double the 20 to get 40.

So, 5 × 8 = 40.

Nines

There's a simple way to work out your nine times table:

> Nasty nines are fine and fun if you
> just fold your fingers and thumbs.

Hold up your hands, with the palms facing you and the fingers spread. The thumb on your left hand is 'one', the index finger is 'two', the middle finger is 'three', and so on, all the way across to the thumb on your right hand, which is 'ten'.

To run through the nine times table, fold the finger that corresponds to the number you are multiplying towards yourself. Any fingers or the thumb to the left of the number finger stand for 'tens', any fingers or the thumb to the right of the number finger stand for 'units'.

Here's how it works:

2 x 9 – fold finger number two (index finger, left hand) towards you, leaving your thumb to the left, representing one, and eight to the right.

If you write out the '1' on the left and the '8' on the right you get: 18. This tells you that $2 \times 9 = 18$.

Let's try 3×9. Fold finger number three (middle finger, left hand) towards you, leaving two fingers to the left and seven to the right. 2 7… 27. So $3 \times 9 = 27$.

Carry on this way and you'll see it works all the way across, with the right hand mirroring the left hand.

The first five answers are 9, 18, 27, 36, 45 – the next five use the same numbers in reverse: 54, 63, 72, 81, 90.

Quick Check. A quick way of checking that your answers to the nine times table are correct is by making sure the numbers in your total always add up to nine:

$$1 \times 9 = 9$$
$$2 \times 9 = 18 \ (1 + 8 = 9)$$
$$3 \times 9 = 27 \ (2 + 7 = 9)$$
$$4 \times 9 = 36 \ (3 + 6 = 9) \text{ and so on.}$$

Check It really works!

Elevens

The first nine multiples of eleven are simple – you always write the same number twice.

So 2 x 11 = 22, 3 x 11 = 33, all the way to 9 x 11 = 99.

Simple, but did you know that there's a sneaky way to work out higher multiples? For example:

> 12 x 11
> 1 + 2 = **3**
> Insert the 3 between the 1 and 2:
> 1**3**2

And if the two digits also add up to a two-digit number:

> Insert the second and add the first.

For example:

> 75 x 11
> 7 + 5 = **12**
> Insert the second digit as before between the 7 and 5:
> 7**2**5
> Then add the first digit to the 7:
> 825

Try it, everyone will think you're a genius.

Twelves

If you find the twelve times table tricky, just use the twos and tens. Two and ten added together make twelve – just add together the same multiple of two and ten to get the right answer for twelve – easy peasy.

And, if you struggle to remember all these rules, try this rhyme as a reminder:

To multiply by two, just double,
To find the threes, you treble.
Four is double, and double again,
Five you just take half of ten.
Times by five, add one for sixes,
For sevens, take five, then two again.
Everyone should know what eight is,
That's right: double, double, double.
Fold fingers for nine, no trouble,
And, for multiples of ten?
Move the numbers one to the left.
Eleven's simple – write it twice,
Using two and ten for twelves is nice.

CONQUER CALCULATIONS

Long Multiplication

What's 12 multiplied by 163? With a calculator you can have the answer in seconds, but what if your calculator breaks? Here's how to do long multiplication.

No matter how large the calculation, you should always start by multiplying the units, followed by tens, then hundreds, and so on. Here's a quick example:

In this calculation, first multiply the 2 by each number above, starting with the units, then tens, then the hundreds (when you multiply the 2 by the 6, remember to carry the 1, and add it to the next column, too):

$$
\begin{array}{r}
1\,6\,3 \\
\times 1\,2 \\
\hline
3\,{}^{1}2\,6 \\
\end{array}
$$

Then write in a zero underneath in the units column before moving on to the tens. Multiply the 1 by each number above, starting with the units, as before:

$$
\begin{array}{r}
1\,6\,3 \\
\times 1\,2 \\
\hline
3\,{}^{1}2\,6 \\
1\,6\,3\,0 \\
\end{array}
$$

Finally, add the two sets of numbers together to find your answer:

$$
\begin{array}{r}
1\,6\,3 \\
\times 1\,2 \\
\hline
3\,\overset{1}{2}\,6 \\
+\ 1\,6\,3\,0 \\
\hline
1\,9\,5\,6 \\
\end{array}
$$

Don't panic, here's a simple acronym to remind you of the correct order to multiply:

Multiply **U**nits **T**ens **H**undreds **A**dd – **MUTHA**.

Long Division

Just as with long multiplication, long division breaks a large calculation into several smaller calculations. So if you need to know how many times 15 goes into 6570, all you'll need is a pen and paper and this mnemonic to find the solution:

Dad, **M**um, **S**ister, **B**rother.

This stands for **D**ivide, **M**ultiply, **S**ubtract, **B**ring down.

Write out the calculation like this: $15\overline{)6570}$

This time starting from the left, see if you can **divide** 15 into the first number. Obviously 15 doesn't go into 6, so you should write a zero directly above it, but if you look at the 6 and 5 as 65, then 15 does fit – four times. Write in 4 next to the zero. Now **multiply** 4 by 15 (60) and write that underneath, then **subtract** 60 from the 65 above, leaving you with 5. Write the 5 underneath:

$$
\begin{array}{r}
0\,4\\
15\overline{)6\,5\,7\,0}\\
6\,0\\
5
\end{array}
$$

Now **bring down** the 7 to sit next to the 5 (57) and go through the steps again. 15 fits into 57 three times (45), with 12 remaining. Lastly bring down the zero to show 120. You can then divide 15 into 120 eight times. Your finished

$$
\begin{array}{r}
0\,4\,3\,8\\
15\overline{)6\,5\,7\,0}\\
-\ \ 6\,0\\
5\,7\\
-\ \ \ \ 4\,5\\
1\,2\,0
\end{array}
$$

Fractions

A fraction is part of a whole number. Fractions such as a half ($\frac{1}{2}$) or a quarter ($\frac{1}{4}$) are made up of two parts, a 'numerator' and a 'denominator'. The denominator tells you how many parts the whole number is divided into; the numerator tells you how many parts you have. For example, the '2' in $\frac{1}{2}$ tells you that the whole number has been divided into two pieces, and the '1' tells you that you have one of them.

When you write a fraction, the numerator goes up above the line; the denominator goes down below it. Remember:

Numerator up, denominator down: Numerator
                                  Denominator

Decimals

Fractions can also be written out as 'decimals'. A half can be written in a fraction as $\frac{1}{2}$ and in a decimal as 0.5. A quarter can be written as $\frac{1}{4}$ or as 0.25.

In the word decimal, 'deci' stands for ten. This helps you remember that the first number to the right of the decimal point shows tenths of a whole number, the next number shows hundredths. Remember:

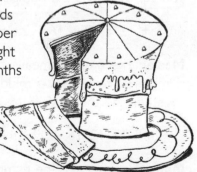

Divide Each Cake Into a DECImal – ten.

Percentages

Percentages **(%)** show the quantity of any number as part of one hundred. The fraction $\frac{1}{2}$ is the same as 50 out of 100, or 50%. Remember:

> Per**cent**ages are like **cent**uries (one hundred years), or **cent**ipedes (which have a hundred legs).

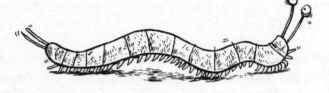

Averages

The average of a group of numbers can be worked out in different ways.

Mean. To work out the 'mean' of a group of numbers, add all the numbers in the group together, then divide the total you get by how many numbers there were. For example:

$$5 + 12 + 12 + 16 + 22 + 23 = 90 \text{ and } 90 \div 6 = \mathbf{15}$$

Median. The 'median', meaning middle, is literally the middle number. If you have two middle numbers, add them together and then divide the total by two. For example:

In 5, 12, **12**, **16**, 22, 23, the average of 12 + 16 is 14.

Mode. The 'mode' is the number that appears most often.

For example, in this set of numbers (5, **12**, **12**, 16, 22, 23), 12 is the mode number. To remember all three try this:

> **Mean** means **a**verage **n**umbers.
> **Medi**an is the **medi**um number.
> **Mo**de occurs **mo**st often.

Square Numbers

If you multiply a number by itself you get a square number. For example, 9 is a square number because 3 x 3 is 9. Instead of writing out that whole sum you can simply write '3^2'. This stands for '3 squared', or 3 multiplied by 3. The small '2' is an '**ind**ex' number – it **ind**icates how many times the number should be multiplied.

Cube Numbers

If you multiply a number by itself, and then by itself again you get a cube number. It's just like multiplying the width of a cube by its height and its depth. 3 x 3 x 3 = 27, so 27 is a cube number, but it can also be written as '3^3'.

Root Numbers

A square root ($\sqrt{\ }$) or a cube root ($\sqrt[3]{\ }$) is the opposite of a squared or a cubed number – it is the number which was originally squared or cubed. The square root of 9 is 3. The cube root of 27 is 3, so:

> Remember the 'root' you used.

MASTER OF MATHS

Prime Numbers

2, 3, 5, 7, 11, 13, 17, 19, 23, 29, 31, 37, 41 …
What do these numbers all have in common? They are
'prime numbers'. Prime numbers are the loners of the
maths world because each one can only be divided by
itself and by 1. Remember:

> **Pri**me numbers are very **pri**vate,
> they only have **one** friend.

Positive and Negative Numbers

On a number line, positive numbers **(+)** are to the right of
the zero. Negative numbers **(–)** are to the left of the zero:

$$-5 \quad -4 \quad -3 \quad -2 \quad -1 \quad 0 \quad 1 \quad 2 \quad 3 \quad 4 \quad 5$$

When you have to multiply positive and negative numbers
together just imagine that the positive numbers are heroes
and the negative numbers are villains:

If a good thing (+) happens to a hero (+), that's good (+):

$$12 \times 12 = 144$$

If a good thing (+) happens to a villain (–), that's bad (–):

$$12 \times -12 = -144$$

If a bad thing (−) happens to a hero (+), that's bad (−):

$$-12 \times 12 = -144$$

If a bad thing (−) happens to a villain (−), that's good (+):

$$-12 \times -12 = 144$$

Usually two wrongs don't make a right, but in this case, they do!

Parallel and Perpendicular

Parallel lines run at the same angle. They never get closer together or further apart, no matter how long they are.

Perpendicular lines meet at an angle of 90 degrees. Use this picture to remember the difference:

Metric Measurements

Length. When measuring the length of something, you need different units of measurement because some lengths are enormous, such as the distance between two countries, and some are tiny, such as the distance between your nostrils.

The 'base' measurement for all metric lengths is the metre. All the other units are based on a metre. They are either larger, such as a kilometre, or smaller, such as a centimetre.

You can always work out which units are larger or smaller than a metre by remembering this acrostic:

King **H**ector's **D**efinitely **M**ad – **D**rinking **C**old **M**ilk.

This stands for:

> **K**ilometre – 1000 metres
> **H**ectometre – 100 metres
> **D**ecametre – 10 metres
> **M**etre – 1 metre
> **D**ecimetre – 0.1 metre
> **C**entimetre – 0.01 metre
> **M**illimetre – 0.001 metre.

Mass. When measuring mass, the base measurement is a gram. Kilograms, grams and milligrams are the ones you will use most, but you can remember them all with this sentence as a reminder:

King Hector's Definitely Going to Decide on Cold Milk.

This stands for:

Kilogram – 1000 grams
Hectogram – 100 grams
Decagram – 10 grams
Gram – 1 gram
Decigram – 0.1 gram
Centigram – 0.01 gram
Milligram – 0.001 gram.

Capacity. If you are measuring liquids, the measurement is based on a litre, so remember:

King Hector's Definitely Likely to Decide on Cold Milk.

Which stands for:

Kilolitre – 1000 litres
Hectolitre – 100 litres
Decalitre – 10 litres
Litre – 1 litre
Decilitre – 0.1 litre
Centilitre – 0.01 litre
Millilitre – 0.001 litre.

STRAIGHTEN OUT GEOMETRY

Angles

Imagine standing on one spot and turning all the way around in a circle. This circle is a full turn of 360 degrees – that's easy to remember because the symbol for degrees is a little circle (°).

A 'right angle' is a quarter of a turn, or 90°. Squares and rectangles have four right angles, adding up to 360°. To remind you of the 'right angle', just think of this:

A capital 'T' has Two right angles.

An angle of less than 90° is called an 'acute' angle and an angle between 90° and 180° is 'obtuse':

> A**cute** angles are thin angles – they're **cute**.
> **Ob**tuse angles are fat angles – they're **ob**ese.

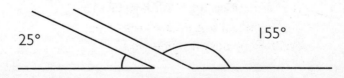

Triangles

The angles of a triangle always add up to 180°. A clever way to confirm this is to cut a triangle out of paper. Trim off all three corners and arrange the corners to form a straight line, which is 180°.

Here are the different types of triangle and ways to remember them:

Equilateral triangle. Just as the name suggests, each side and each angle are exactly **equal**.

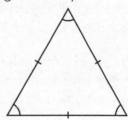

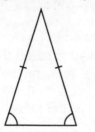

Isosceles triangle. These always have two sides and two angles of equal size and look rather like a Christmas tree.

The song, 'Oh Christmas Tree', has been reworded to help you remember:

> Isosceles, Isosceles,
> *(Oh, Christmas Tree, Oh Christmas Tree,)*
> Two angles have equal degrees.
> *(How lovely are your branches.)*
> Isosceles, Isosceles,
> *(Oh, Christmas Tree, Oh Christmas Tree,)*
> You look just like a Christmas tree.
> *(With happiness we greet you.)*

Scalene triangle.
This is the only triangle
where each side and
each angle is different.

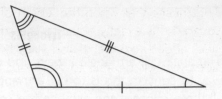

Pythagorean Theorem

This is a right-angled triangle:

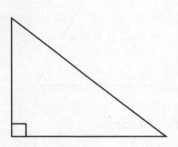

A right-angled triangle can be
isosceles or scalene, but it
always has one angle of exactly
90° – a right angle.

The longest side of a right-
angled triangle is called the
'hypotenuse'. Remember:

The hypotenuse is the longest word for the longest side.

The hypotenuse is always
the side opposite the right
angle. The Greek
mathematician, Pythagoras,
worked out that:

'The square of the
hypotenuse is equal to
the sum of the squares
of the other two sides.'

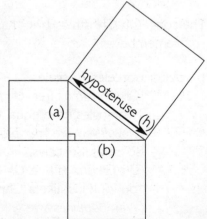

This means that when the length of the hypotenuse is squared it is exactly equal to the square of the other two sides added together. If you already know the length of two sides, you will be able to work out the length of the other side using this formula:

$$a^2 + b^2 = h^2$$

Area

Area is the space inside a flat, two-dimensional shape. Think of a field surrounded by fences – the area is the amount of ground inside the fences.

Area is shown using the same symbol you use for square numbers (see page 107). So for example, a field measuring 20 metres by 50 metres is 1000 m². Remember:

Area is always two-dimensional – 2 'a's mean '2D'!

To work out the area of a triangle, first measure its height by drawing a line from the base to the top point. The line must be perpendicular to the base – at a 90° angle.

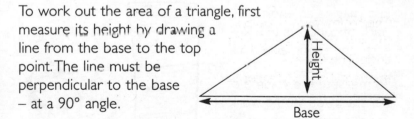

Multiply this measurement by the length of the base. This gives you the area of a quadrilateral, a four-sided shape, which the triangle fits into twice, so remember to divide it by 2. Here is the formula:

$$\frac{base \times height}{2}$$

Volume

Volume is a measurement of the space inside a three-dimensional shape, such as a cup or a swimming pool.

Cuboid. It's easy enough to find the volume of a simple cuboid, or box-like, shape. Just multiply the length by the height and then by the width. So a box measuring 5 cm by 10 cm by 20 cm would have a volume of 1000 cm^3.

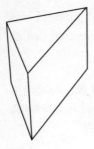

Prisms and Cylinders. But what about more complicated shapes such as prisms, which have a triangular base, or cylinders, which have a circular base? Simple – first work out the area taken up by either the triangle (see page 115) or the circle (see opposite page), then multiply that by the height:

Base × Height.

Just imagine an enormous stack of pancakes that are each one centimetre thick.

To measure the volume of the stack you would work out the area of a pancake and multiply the answer by the number of pancakes in the stack.

Perimeter

Every two-dimensional shape has a perimeter. This is the measurement around its edge or 'rim'. Don't forget:

Perimeter.

Circles

Circumference. This is the distance around a circle. The word gives you a clue:

Only a **circ**le has a **circ**umference.

Radius. This is the line measuring directly from the centre of a circle to its edge. It is like one spoke of a bicycle wheel:

Spokes **radi**ate along the **radi**us.

Diameter. This is the width of a circle, from the edge, through the centre, to the opposite side. It is twice the length of the radius:

Diameter is **d**ouble

It's easy enough to work out the area of a square or a rectangle, but how do you work out the area of a circle? It's as easy as 'π' (pi).

Pi (π) = 3.14. It is the number that will help you work out the area and the circumference of a circle. It's easy to remember, because 3 + 1 = 4.

To find the area of a circle, use this formula:

$$\pi r^2$$
(π × radius squared, or 'Pi r squared')

This means that you multiply the radius (r) by itself (^{2}), then multiply that number by π. If the radius is 5 cm, the radius squared is 25 cm. This number multiplied by π is 78.5 cm^2, so the area of the circle is 78.5 cm^2. To remember the formula just think:

Some **A**pple pies (π!) are square (^{2}): **A**rea.

To find the circumference of a circle, use the formula:

$$\pi d$$

This means that you need to multiply the diameter (d) by π. If the radius of a circle is 5 cm, the diameter must be 10 cm, and 10 × π = 31.4 cm. Remember:

Cherry pie (π!) is **d**elicious: **C**ircumference.

The simplest form of π is 3.14, but it is really an infinite number, impossible to calculate precisely. Here is a party trick that will really impress people – use this rhyme to remember π to the first 20 decimal places. The number of letters in each word matches the digit at each decimal place:

> Now, I wish I could recollect pi.
> 'Eureka', cried the great inventor.
> Christmas Pudding, Christmas Pie,
> Is the problem's very centre.

(3.14159265358979323846)

OUT OF
SCHOOL

GENERAL KNOWLEDGE

Here are some useful tips and hints to remind you of lots of things you might not learn at school.

Left and Right

This might seem super-simple, but some people really struggle to tell their left from their right. Here's a subtle way to remind yourself (when no one is looking). Just hold your hands out in front of you, palms down, with the thumbs sticking out sideways. Your left hand will make the shape of a capital 'L' – handy!

Opening Lids

This easy mnemonic makes sure you remember which way to turn a screw to loosen it and which way to tighten it. It also works brilliantly when opening and closing jam-jar lids!

Lefty loosey,
Righty tighty.

Riding a Bike

If you're learning to ride a bike, the most important thing to know is how to use your brakes to stop.

The right brake connects to the front wheel and the left brake to the rear wheel. Always squeeze the left brake to stop the rear wheel first, then squeeze the right brake. If you squeeze both brakes together – or, worse, if you only squeeze the right brake – you're likely to go flying over the handlebars.

When you get going, pedalling happily and keeping your balance, make sure you fix your gaze ahead, and don't look down. You'll find it much easier to keep steady and you're less likely to cycle into a tree, too. So, always remember:

> Brakes before balance,
> Left before right,
> Don't look down!

Learn How to Tie a Tie

Put the tie around your neck with your shirt collar up. Imagine the wide side is a 'rabbit', and the narrow side is a 'fence' – all you need to remember is:

> Over, under, around and through.

First take the rabbit over the fence, then under the fence, then all the way around. Lastly bring it up through the middle then down through the loop you have made. Ta da!

Life-Saving Techniques

If someone is unconscious, these checkpoints can really help while you wait for an ambulance to arrive – saving a life can be as simple as **ABC**:

> **A**irway
> **B**reathing
> **C**irculation.

First, make certain the person's **A**irway is open by tilting their chin back a little. Check to make sure nothing is blocking their mouth and throat.

Then check for signs of **B**reathing. Is their chest rising and falling? Can you hear them breathing? If not, put your cheek or ear against their mouth: you might be able to feel their breath.

Lastly, check **C**irculation by feeling for a pulse in their neck or at the wrist, to make sure their heart is beating.

Survival Tips

The three essentials of survival are:

    Shelter – provides protection against bad weather.
    Water – thirst leads to exhaustion faster than hunger.
    Food – hunger is slow to kill, but lowers your spirits.

If you have those, you can **S**urvive **W**ithout **F**ear!

Human survival is ruled by the number three – you cannot survive longer than:

        Three minutes without oxygen,
        Three hours at freezing temperatures,
        Three days without water,
        Three weeks without food.

Port and Starboard

On board a ship, 'port' is the left side of the ship and 'starboard' is the right side. An easy way to remember this is that both 'port' and 'left' have four letters, and that 'starboard' and 'right' both have more than four letters.

The Animal World

Camels. There are two kinds of camel – the dromedary and the Bactrian. The dromedary has one hump, like a capital D turned on its side: ∩. The Bactrian has two humps, like a capital B turned on its side: ∞.

Elephants. There are African elephants and Indian elephants. Africa is larger than India, and African elephants are bigger than Indian elephant, with larger ears, too.

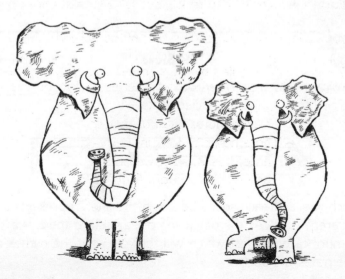

MUSICAL MAESTRO

If you know the alphabet, you already know a little bit about music, because the notes are named after the first seven letters of the alphabet, from '**A**' to '**G**'.

The Stave

Musical notes are written out as a series of dots on five parallel lines, which are called a 'stave':

Each line, and each space between the lines, represents a different 'note'. At the beginning of each stave there is a symbol called a 'clef', which will tell you what the names of the notes will be.

Treble Clef

The 'treble clef' (𝄞) is used by musical instruments that have a high sound, such as the recorder and the violin. It is also used for the higher notes on the piano (the notes that are played with a pianist's right hand).

Starting from the bottom, the notes that appear on each line are **E**, **G**, **B**, **D** and **F**. Just remember:

Every **G**ood **B**oy **D**eserves **F**avour.

The notes that sit in the spaces between each line are **F**, **A**, **C** and **E**. Just remember:

A note in a space
Is as plain as your **FACE**.

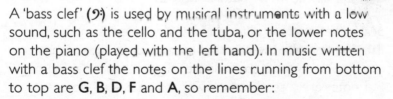

Bass Clef

A 'bass clef' (𝄢) is used by musical instruments with a low sound, such as the cello and the tuba, or the lower notes on the piano (played with the left hand). In music written with a bass clef the notes on the lines running from bottom to top are **G**, **B**, **D**, **F** and **A**, so remember:

Good **B**oys **D**on't **F**ool **A**round.

The notes sitting in the spaces in bass clef are **A**, **C**, **E** and **G**. Just think:

All **C**ats **E**at **G**oldfish.

Scales

Eight notes, played in order, make up a 'scale'. The starting note in a scale is called the '**tonic**'. Remember:

The first note always sounds right, like a **tonic** for your ears.

The tonic of a scale gives the scale its name. The tonic of C major, for instance, is C.

These are the notes in C major: C, D, E, F, G, A, B, C.

These eight notes make up an 'octave'. The notes at either end of the scale are both C but one sounds higher than the other. Remember:

An **oct**opus has **eight** arms – an **oct**ave has **eight** notes.

C major is the simplest scale to learn because you do not have to sharpen (raise) or flatten (lower) any of the notes – they are all known as 'natural' notes.

Scales that start on different notes do need sharps (♯) or flats (♭) to make them sound correct, or 'in tune'. A sharp note is a 'semi-tone' (half a note) higher than a natural note. Flat notes are a semi-tone lower than a natural note. A semi-tone sounds halfway between one note and the next. Remember:

A **semi**-circle is half a circle – a **semi**-tone is half a note.

The sharps and flats added to a scale make up the 'key signature' – they are 'key' to making the scale sound correct.

Just as colours that do not go together can make you wince, an out-of-tune scale, with notes that do not go together, can do the same.

___

Key Signatures

Groups of sharps or flats next to the clef tell you what key signature to play a piece of music in. A sharp (♯) or a flat (♭) on a particular line or space will change the sound of that note, making it half a note higher or lower.

Sharps. The first scale with a sharp added to it is G major. The F in G major is sharp and is written F♯. G is a 'fifth' higher than C (the five notes from C to G – C, D, E, F and G – are a fifth). Go up another fifth, to D major, and you will need two sharps – F♯ and C♯. Another sharp is added to scales each time in this order: **F♯, C♯, G♯, D♯, A♯, E♯** and **B♯**. You can remember them like this:

Father Charles Goes Down And Ends Battle.

Flats. Other key signatures have flats instead of sharps. Starting with F major, which has one flat, this time move up in 'fourths', to B♭ major, which has two flats, then E♭ major, which has three, and so on. Flats are added to scales in this order: **B♭, E♭, A♭, D♭, G♭, C♭** and **F♭**. Use this to remember them:

Battle Ends And Down Goes Charles's Father.

Simple.